1. THE FEUDAL SYSTEM

After the barbarians invaded the Roman Empire, many wars were fought. The winners were those who were strongest and most clever. Gradually, the winners became kings of large areas. They gathered other strong men around them. You will learn how the land was divided and the system that was used to maintain control.

Section Objectives

Review these objectives. When you have completed this section, you should be able to:

1. Describe the basic plan of feudalism.
2. List ways that Christianity has improved the lives of poor people.

Vocabulary

Study these words to enhance your learning success in this section.

barbarian (bär ber′ ē un). A person belonging to a people or tribe that is not civilized.

fief (fēf). Land held in exchange for service.

granary (grā′ nur ē). A place where grain is stored.

manor (man′ ur). A feudal estate.

serf (serf). Person owned by a landowner. He could not be sold away from land.

thatched (thacht). Roofed with straw.

vassal (vas′ ul). One who is a subject of a lord.

villein (vil′ un). One of the lower class in the feudal system, obligated to the lord, but free in other ways.

Note: *All vocabulary words in this LIFEPAC appear in* **boldface** *print the first time they are used. If you are not sure of the meaning when you are reading, study the definitions given.*

Pronunciation Key: hat, āge, cãre, fär; let, ēqual, tėrm; it, īce; hot, ōpen, ôrder; oil; out; cup, pu̇t, rüle; child; long; thin; /ϜH/ for then; /zh/ for measure; /u/ or /ə/ represents /a/ in about, /e/ in taken, /i/ in pencil, /o/ in lemon, and /u/ in circus.

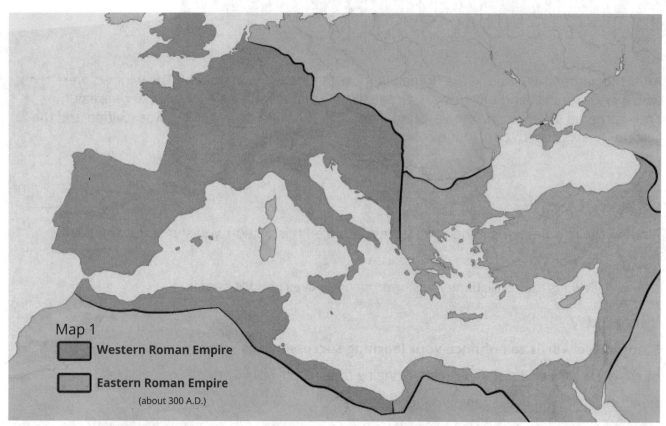

Map 1

Western Roman Empire

Eastern Roman Empire

(about 300 A.D.)

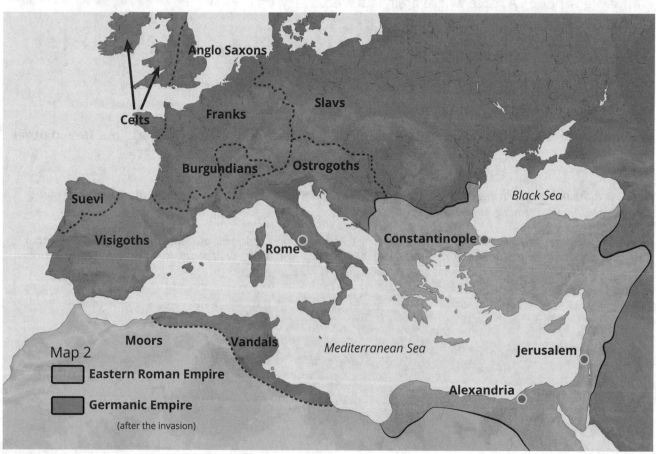

Anglo Saxons

Celts

Franks

Slavs

Burgundians

Ostrogoths

Suevi

Black Sea

Visigoths

Rome

Constantinople

Moors

Vandals

Mediterranean Sea

Jerusalem

Alexandria

Map 2

Eastern Roman Empire

Germanic Empire

(after the invasion)

HISTORY & GEOGRAPHY 604
Life in the Middle Ages

LIFEPAC Test is located in the center of the booklet. Please remove before starting the unit.

Author:
Ethel Hofflund, M.A.

Editor-in-Chief:
Richard W. Wheeler, M.A.Ed.

Editor:
Elizabeth Loeks Bouman

Consulting Editor:
Howard Stitt, Th.M., Ed.D.

Revision Editor:
Alan Christopherson, M.S.

MEDIA CREDITS:
Page 9: © John Gollop, iStock, Thinkstock; **20:** © Sylphe_7, iStock, Thinkstock; **25:** © Shaiith, iStock, Thinkstock; **52:** © Angela Farley, iStock, Thinkstock; **59:** (left) © kremez, iStock, Thinkstock; (right) © Hemera Technologies, AbleStock.com, Thinkstock.

Alpha Omega
PUBLICATIONS

804 N. 2nd Ave. E.
Rock Rapids, IA 51246-1759

Life in the Middle Ages

Introduction

You have studied about the Roman Empire, which existed in Christ's time. Rome had wealth and power. Rome was a center of learning and worldly strength, but it became weak morally. Gradually, the civilized world was destroyed by the barbarians from the north. Violence continued for a thousand years. You will enjoy this LIFEPAC® study because you will learn about knights and castles, towns, and fairs. You will learn about the food, the recreation, and the dress of those times. When you have finished, see if you can determine how mankind can avoid another "dark age."
(Christ is the "Light" of the world.)

Objectives

Read these objectives. The objectives tell you what you will be able to do when you have successfully completed this LIFEPAC. When you have finished this LIFEPAC, you should be able to:

1. Describe the basic plan of feudalism.

2. List ways that Christianity has improved the lives of underprivileged people.

3. Describe the habits, foods, dress, and pleasures of the people who lived in the Middle Ages.

4. Explain the debt we owe the scholars of the Middle Ages.

5. Compare schools of today with those of the Middle Ages.

6. Describe the beliefs, origin, and culture of Islam.

7. List the reasons for and the results of the Crusades.

8. Explain what we can learn from the Crusades.

9. Describe the growth of towns and trade.

10. Explain the need for guilds.

11. Describe markets and fairs.

12. Explain the importance of the Catholic Church in the Middle Ages.

13. Explain the role of religious drama.

Survey the LIFEPAC. Ask yourself some questions about this study and write your questions here.

_____
_____
_____
_____
_____
_____
_____
_____
_____
_____
_____
_____
_____
_____
_____
_____
_____
_____

THE BARBARIAN INVASION

Rome had ruled the civilized Western World for about 400 years. The Roman Empire included western Asia, northern Africa, and the land west of the Rhine River and south of the Danube River. The Visigoths, Franks, Angles, and Saxons were barbaric tribes that lived in the forest, north of the Danube River. In contrast to the dark-complexioned races of the Mediterranean, the **barbarians** were blonde. These strong, but unlearned, barbarians conquered the civilized, educated, wealthy, and powerful Romans. The Roman Empire fell apart. How could this happen? Rome had wealth and power. Rome was a center of learning and strength, but it was weak *morally*. Rome was poor *spiritually*. Both the leaders and the people put their trust in their wealth and power. They began to live for selfish purposes. Self-discipline weakened. Most of the people fell into sinful ways. The Empire's authority and power drained away.

The barbarous tribes north of the Danube had never been conquered by Rome. They took the opportunity of Rome's weakening control to filter across the Danube. They gained support from tribes south of the Danube that had not been completely subdued by Rome. Together, they invaded and overran most of the Western Roman Empire.

The barbarians brought violence and destruction everywhere they went. For more than a thousand years, between A.D. 395 and A.D. 1500, little government and few schools could be found. People lived in ignorance and danger. Those years are known as the Middle Ages. The first five centuries are known as the Dark Ages.

Gradually, the barbarians who had invaded the Roman Empire learned from the Romans. A new way of life rose from the ruins of the older civilization, but it happened slowly and unevenly. In each district, the strongest man came to be the leader and protector. During most of the Middle Ages, many kings ruled over small kingdoms.

Write the correct letter on each blank.

1.1 The Roman Empire included _____ .
a. half of the world today b. very little of the world today

1.2 Study Map 2. The city of Rome was located _____ .
a. near the center of the empire b. on the western border

1.3 Study Map 2. Western civilization was located around _____ .
a. the Black Sea b. the Mediterranean Sea

1.4 The barbarians lived _____ .
a. south of the Danube b. north of the Danube

1.5 Rome ruled the civilized Western world for _____ .
a. hundreds of years b. thousands of years

Name the invading tribes (use Map 2).

1.6 _____

1.7 _____

1.8 _____

1.9 _____

1.10 _____

1.11 _____

1.12 _____

Unscramble the words and write the new words on the lines.

elargnin   dimdle egsa

1.13 Almost all _____ was destroyed.

1.14 This period in history is known as the _____ .

Read Galatians 3:28.   If you don't understand the verse, talk it over with another student or with your teacher.

As you study the next section, think about what Paul said. What was good and what was wrong in the feudal system?

THE SYSTEM OF LAND OWNERSHIP

Naturally, each king claimed all the land in his kingdom, but he gave some of the land to the lords or nobles who fought for him. These land gifts were called **manors**. Then the nobles gave some of their land to **vassals**. The vassals then owed nobles certain duties. The lands of vassals were called **fiefs**. This system of land ownership and duties was called the feudal system. Taxes have been required by rulers from Bible times to modern times. During feudalism, taxes were not paid in money, but in products and in services. Tributes (gifts and taxes) were required by the lords from their vassals. No new taxes could be levied without the consent of the vassals. At harvest time, the vassals gave shares of their crops to the lords. The vassals would grind their grain at the nobles' **granaries**.

| A manor had to support many people.

They would give part of the grain to their lord (noble). When animals were slaughtered for food, part of the meat was given to the lords. In return, the lords promised protection, peace, and security.

Manors were completely owned by the nobles and were passed on from one generation to another. The noble's first-born son inherited all. If there were no son, a daughter took possession. Each manor had its own pasture lands, mill, wine press, church, and village. A manor had to support many people. If food ran out, a noble might move his entire household to another manor where conditions were more favorable. A noble gave his servants food and lodging, but did not pay them money.

The **villein** belonged to the poorer class. He was obligated to the lords, but free in his other relationships. He had work to do for the lord or the town, then he returned to his little hut with earthen floors and a **thatched** roof. On the walls of the hut, the villein hung meats, tools, and dried vegetables. He cooked his meals over a fire in the middle of the floor.

Perhaps the next day he would help mend a bridge or road. All the people depended upon each other, but the manor itself was an independent community.

A villein was better off than the slaves or **serfs**, but sometimes he longed to be totally free. He could not even leave the manor lands without permission from the lord of the manor. If he escaped, he could flee to a town where he would try to live quietly and unknown for a year and a day. If he succeeded, he was a free man. If he preferred to enter the service of the Catholic Church, he had to secure special permission. As a member of the church, he could rise above his low position in society. However, if he were unsuccessful in his choice, he had one alternative left: he could join a band of outlaws. He had to choose wisely because in those days punishment of outlaws was severe.

The serf was in the lowest class of all. He was little better than a slave. He could not be sold away from the land, but was always sold with the land.

Write what was good and what was wrong about the feudal system.

1.15 GOOD

_____

_____

_____

1.16 WRONG

_____

_____

_____

Complete the following sentences.

1.17 The lords who fought for the king were given _____ .

1.18 The lords gave lands to _____ .

1.19 This system of land ownership was called the _____ system.

Answer the following questions.

1.20 How were taxes paid during feudalism? _____

1.21 The lord had to promise his vassals three things. What were they?

a. _____   b. _____   c. _____

1.22 What were the three choices a villein had to be able to become a free man?

a. _____

b. _____

c. _____

Answer true or false.

1.23 _____ The neighboring lord inherited the manor.

1.24 _____ A manor was mainly farmland with very few people.

1.25 _____ Villeins were the poor people who were semi-free.

1.26 _____ If food ran out, a noble might sell his property to serfs to pay for food.

1.27 _____ A villein could enter the service of the church with the permission of the lord.

Complete this activity.

1.28 Write five sentences about underprivileged people: people that struggle with money, social status, or work conditions. How did Jesus feel about these people?
How are the underprivileged helped in our country and what more can we do to help?

_____

_____

_____

_____

_____

_____

_____

_____

Review the material in this section in preparation for the Self Test. The Self Test will check your mastery of this particular section. The items missed on this Self Test will indicate specific areas where restudy is needed for mastery.

SELF TEST 1

Answer these questions (each answer, 3 points).

1.01   To whom did the lord give land? _____

1.02   To whom did the vassals pledge allegiance? _____

1.03   What is the name of the system of land ownership in the Middle Ages? _____

1.04   Who made up the lowest class of people in the feudal system? _____

1.05   Besides security and peace, what else did the lords promise? _____

1.06   What were the lands on which the lords lived called? _____

1.07   Who gave the lords this land? _____

1.08   Who were the villeins? _____

_____

1.09   What could the lord do if food ran out? _____

_____

1.010 Name one way a villein could become totally free. _____

_____

Answer true or false (each answer, 2 points).

1.011   _____   Villeins could live very comfortably.

1.012   _____   A first-born son inherited all of the manor.

1.013   _____   Villeins went to their own homes at night.

1.014   _____   Nobles gave land to the king.

1.015   _____   Barbarians north of the Danube invaded the Roman Empire.

1.016   _____   Ostrogoths were a barbarian tribe.

1.017   _____   Many kings ruled over small kingdoms.

1.018   _____   Nobles could levy taxes without the consent of anyone.

1.019   _____   A fief was a man who was practically a slave.

1.020   _____   A villein could enter the service of the church with special permission.

Answer these questions in complete sentences (each answer, 4 points).

1.021 Name four barbaric tribes (1 point for each tribe). _____

_____

1.022 Why did the barbaric tribes conquer Rome? _____

_____

1.023 What were two ways people paid their taxes under the feudal system? _____

_____

_____

1.024 What were the conditions that led to the development of the feudal system? _____

_____

_____

1.025 How was a manor independent of all other manors? _____

_____

Match these items (each correct match, 3 points).

1.026 _____ Visigoth   a. vassal

1.027 _____ thatched hut   b. belonged to the land

1.028 _____ feudalism   c. noble

1.029 _____ fief   d. mended bridges

1.030 _____ outlaw   e. promised protection

1.031 _____ taxes   f. barbarian

1.032 _____ manor   g. villein

1.033 _____ serf   h. system of land ownership

1.034 _____ villein   i. severe punishment

1.035 _____ lord   j. products and services

80 / 100   **SCORE** _____   **TEACHER** _____ _____
                                                    initials   date

2. THE DAILY LIFE

The daily life in the castle during the Middle Ages naturally varied greatly from life in the **hovel**. Yet some things were the same for everyone. You will learn that the kind of food eaten in a castle or manor house differed greatly from that eaten in a serf 's hut. You will learn that sanitation and medicine were very primitive for all classes of people. You will also learn some unusual ways of managing daily activities.

Section Objectives

Review these objectives. When you have completed this section, you should be able to:

2. List ways that Christianity has improved the life of underprivileged people.

3. Describe the habits, food, dress, and pleasures of the people who lived in the Middle Ages.

Vocabulary

Study these words to enhance your learning success in this section.

Crusade (krü sād′). A Catholic military expedition to the Holy Land to recapture it from the Muslims.

hovel (huv′ ul). A small, poorly built house or hut.

moat (mōt). A deep, wide ditch surrounding a castle.

motte (mot). A mound upon which a wood castle was built.

plumbing (plum′ ing). The water pipes and fixtures in a building.

portcullis (pôrt kul′ is). A sliding metal grating to be lowered in front of the door of the castle.

quarantine (kwôr′ un ten). To isolate.

scullion (skul′ yun). A servant who does the dirty, rough work in a kitchen.

sundial (sun′ di ul). An instrument that indicates time by the position of the shadow.

toga (tō′ gu). A loose robe worn by Romans.

Pronunciation Key: hat, āge, cãre, fär; let, ēqual, tėrm; it, īce; hot, ōpen, ôrder; oil; out; cup, púk, rüle; child; long; thin; /ŦH/ for then; /zh/ for measure; /u/ or /ə/ represents /a/ in about, /e/ in taken, /i/ in pencil, /o/ in lemon, and /u/ in circus.

| Diagram showing the main parts of a castle

1 Banner
2 Watchtower
3 Postern
4 Donjon
5 Outer Bailey
6 Inner Bailey
7 Lord's Home
8 Courtyard
9 Chapel
10 Well
11 Curtains
12 Towers
13 Hourds
14 Portcullis
15 Kitchen
16 Drawbridge
17 Moat
18 Motte
19 Gate
20 Barriers
21 Villeins Homes

CASTLES

The king and the lords lived in great castles during the Middle Ages. Some of those castles can still be seen. At one time, England alone had 300 castles. Each castle was built in a way that would protect its inhabitants. In times of attack, the farm workers and villagers hurried to the castle for safety. Then everyone helped fight the aggressor. The towers, from which men looked over the landscape, were often seventy feet (21 meters) high. The walls were eight feet (2.5 meters) thick. Surrounding the castle was a motte (a mound of earth) and a moat (a ditch of water). To cross the water, a drawbridge had to be let down and a portcullis raised. Doors were built of solid oak.

Daily activities. The daily life at a castle was much like ours in some ways, but very unlike ours in others. Walls were white-washed once a year to cover the dirt. The clocks were unreliable because they were **sundials** or hourglasses. Clothes were kept in chests. Everyone rose at daybreak and went to bed at sunset. Candles, oil lamps, and torches were usually the only sources of light after sunset. Beds usually had canopies. People did wash, but bathed only once a week. The soap used was made from wood ashes and mutton (sheep) fat.

The lord shaved with a pumice stone. Prayers were said when they knelt in the bedroom. A lady had a maid help her braid her hair and put on clothes before she began work for the day. Her tasks often included checking the supplies.

Recreation. A lady's recreation was unlike that of today. A lady went for a walk in the garden or played an early form of badminton called "Shuttlecock and Battledore." She could ride in a carriage, or sometimes on horseback, if the kingdom was not at war.

Young girls played with dolls. When girls were old enough, they learned their lessons in the castle, but the boys and men went outside for archery, javelin throwing, or hunting. Boys were trained for fighting when they were seven or eight. The big meal of the day was served at about five in the afternoon.

Because most people could not read and few books were available for those who could read, the people listened to each other narrate legends. Good stories were in great demand. Belief in monsters and witchcraft remained even among those who considered themselves Christian. History and fantasy were often mixed in stories that are known as "folklore."

 Complete the following statements.

2.1 The lord shaved with a _____ .

2.2 Walls were whitewashed every year because _____ .

2.3 Clothes were kept in a _____ .

2.4 People slept in beds that had _____ .

2.5 Everyone went to bed at sunset because _____

_____ .

2.6 People bathed at least _____ .

2.7 Supper was served so early in the evening because _____ .

2.8 Prayers were said at _____ .

CLOTHING

When the barbarians invaded the Roman Empire, the men of the Roman Empire wore **togas**, which were loose, flowing robes. Gradually, after the barbarian invasion, trousers replaced the togas. Fabrics were made of coarse material until the Europeans went on the **Crusades** and discovered softer and more beautiful materials. Shoes were sandals or moccasins. For shirts, the men wore tunics.

Often, they used belts to carry a pouch, a sword, and a dagger. The upper classes wore cloaks which were very full capes with fur at the collars. Wealthy ladies wore long, full dresses with full sleeves. Toward the end of the period, they had silk fabrics and wide embroidered belts called girdles. The lower classes still wore the coarse materials. Children wore clothing similar to that worn by their parents.

Complete the following statements.

2.9 At the time of the invasion, Roman men were wearing loose robes called _____ .

2.10 New fabrics were discovered when people went on the _____ to the Holy Land.

2.11 Men began to wear an article of clothing that both men and women wear today. This article of clothing is called _____ .

2.12 Women wore dresses with sleeves that were _____ .

FOOD

Food was very precious in the Middle Ages. Remember that they had no supermarkets where they could secure more supplies if they ran out. For breakfast, only a piece of bread was served. For the poor, supper was served at about five in the afternoon, and was usually bread, soup, meat or fish, and perhaps some vegetables. The wealthy people had three-course meals. The first course included meats; the second course, meat and pie; the third course, meat, pie, fish, and eggs. Sometimes vegetables were also served. Apples, pears, or plums might be eaten when fruits were available. Spices included ginger, cloves, pepper, nutmeg, and cinnamon. They were often used to hide the spoilage of meat. Salt was used to preserve meats and to flavor food. In fact, the salt container divided the upper class from the lower class.

All the food was prepared by servants under the guidance of the cook. To avoid fires, the kitchen was apart from the castle.

Scullions kept the fires going and meat turning on spits. A miller ground flour, and a baker added his skill by making barley cakes and pastries, which used fish and meat. Honey was used for sweetening because it was available on the manor. Fish that are rarely eaten by us were considered delicacies. These fish delicacies included pikes, eels, and carp.

Such meats as swans, peacocks, and partridges were also considered delicacies. They drank wine, apple cider, ale, and milk.

Eating and drinking were favorite pastimes. Many dinner parties were held.

The guests were seated at the proper tables for the evening meal. A page helped in the hand-washing ceremony. After the guests had washed their hands, a trumpet sounded, and the pages brought in the food. The food was carried a long distance from the kitchen and often cooled off. At Easter or Christmas great feasts were held. At times the meals included ten courses. Although many of the foods were like ours, other things were not. People had knives and spoons, but no forks. Carvers cut the meat into pieces. Squires and pages had to bring in the pitchers, basins, and napkins. The table decoration was the saltcellar, a large dish, often made of silver.

The most startling kind of event that might happen would not be likely now. A cook might serve a pie and put in live birds at the last minute so that when the pie was opened the birds would begin to fly or sing.

Remember the old nursery rhyme, "Sing a Song of Sixpence"? This old nursery rhyme describes birds flying out of a king's pie.

Answer the following questions.

2.13 How did the food compare with what you eat?

_____

_____

_____

2.14 Why do you think water was not used more often for washing or drinking?

_____

_____

_____

Complete the following statements.

2.15 Using salt divided the a. _____ from the b. _____ .

2.16 Spices that were used included a. _____ , b. _____ ,

c. _____ , d. _____ , and e. _____ .

2.17 The kitchen was _____ from the castle because of the danger of fire.

2.18 The guests were assisted by _____ during the hand-washing ceremony.

2.19 The meat was cut into small pieces by _____ .

2.20 Meats eaten that we seldom eat included a. _____ , b. _____ ,

and c. _____ .

2.21 The most popular drinks were a. _____ b. _____ ,

c. _____ , and d. _____ .

SANITATION

Homes were very primitive by our standards. Even an outdoor toilet was a luxury. Most poor people had a hole in the middle of the floor for a toilet. In London, garbage was thrown in the streets until the fourteenth century. Underground **plumbing** was poor until the 1200s. Open fires were used, and the smoke blackened the walls. Mud was used to fill in cracks in wooden houses. Thieves often entered by knocking out the mud. Dirt floors were common and roofs were thatched. Homes were rough, indeed. Life was hard for the lower classes and underprivileged.

Read Matthew 25:34 - 40.

Answer these two questions.

2.22 If you believe what these verses say, what would you have done to help the underprivileged people in the Middle Ages? What can you do today?

_____

_____

_____

_____

Write the correct letter and answer on each blank.

2.23 One luxury few poor people had was _____ .
    a. a thatched roof   b. an outdoor toilet   c. open fires

2.24 Homes could not be kept clean because of the _____ .
    a. lack of brushes   b. smallness of rooms   c. open fires

2.25 Because mud was used in houses, _____ .
    a. thieves could enter easily   b. bricks were seldom used   c. ventilation was good

2.26 The best kind of plumbing is _____ .
    a. an open sewage system   b. a system of pipes   c. ditches

Complete this activity.

2.27 Rewrite the root using any letters that have been dropped.
    The _root_ of a word is the main part of the word. It does not include the prefix or the suffix of these words. An example is given.

	WORD		ROOT
	ignoble		noble

a. supermarket _____

b. wonderful _____

c. inadequate _____

d. impossible _____

e. pruning _____

f. cherished _____

g. confessions _____

h. aristocratic _____

i. nobly _____

j. knighthood _____

k. portcullis _____

l. procedure _____

m. attacker _____

n. ceremonial _____

HEALTH

Modernized medicine was in its infancy. Some attempts were made to heal people. Many people who tried to treat the sick were not qualified. Some medieval doctors secured "treatments" from the Arabs, but many people clung to their superstitions and "cures." Other people argued that sickness was willed on them by God. However, when a plague broke out, most people knew they should avoid contact with the sick; consequently, thousands fled from the disease-ridden, rat-infested cities.

Because of greater cleanliness, purer water, and preventative medicine, most of us have never known the ravages of the numerous diseases common to the Middle Ages. Besides the plagues that destroyed entire cities, other diseases were smallpox, diphtheria, tetanus, influenza, and leprosy. Epidemics were common. To prevent disease from spreading, the city of Venice passed a **quarantine** law, requiring the sick to remain isolated from others, and also requiring the dead to be buried outside the city.

Most young people today have helped to clean up some form of pollution. Pollution has always been a problem for man. Pollution existed during and prior to the Middle Ages. After the barbarian invasion, Roman health laws declined and human suffering resulted from the filth. Gradually, health laws returned. Paris even paved its streets in 1185 to make the city cleaner. By 1309, London had passed an ordinance that prevented inhabitants from throwing garbage into the streets and sometimes on the head of a passerby. Precious water routes could no longer be contaminated with dyes used for coloring clothing.

| Water routes needed to be free of pollution.

Discuss with a classmate the reasons laws for cleanliness must be passed when everyone is affected by pollution. Discuss new rules that you think should be made.

Answer these questions.

2.28 Why do you think cities had plagues? _____
_____

2.29 Why do we have fewer diseases today? _____
_____

2.30 What city originated the quarantine law? _____

2.31 What have you done to help clean up some form of pollution? _____
_____

2.32 If you were an adult hired to inspect food or water or factories, whom would you excuse from obeying the laws? _____

Write a short essay.

2.33 On a separate paper write two or three paragraphs about pollution. Mention problems of the Middle Ages and some of today's problems. Tell what people did then to help and what we have done or should do today to prevent pollution.

Complete the following activities.

2.34 Adjectives are made from proper nouns by adding suffixes.
An example is:

proper noun	adjective	meaning
Christ	Christian	that which is like Christ

Use the following suffixes to complete this exercise: *ian* (pertaining to); *ical* (pertaining to); *ern* (belonging to); *ish* (belonging to); *an* (of, or pertaining to).

Proper Noun	Adjective	Meaning of Adjective
Castile	a. _____	f. _____
Spain	b. _____	g. _____
Rome	c. _____	h. _____
West	d. _____	i. _____
Bible	e. _____	j. _____

2.35 Write these words in correct alphabetical order. Begin with the first letter that is different. The first one is done for you. (The prefix *bene* pertains to a kindness or a blessing.)

benefaction   a. _____ Benedict _____

Benedict   b. _____

Benedictinism   c. _____

benediction   d. _____

benedictional   e. _____

benefactress   f. _____

beneficial   g. _____

beneficiary   h. _____

benedictionary   i. _____

Benedictine   j. _____

↺   **Review the material in this section in preparation for the Self Test.** This Self Test will check your mastery of this particular section as well as your knowledge of the previous section.

SELF TEST 2

Choose the correct answer and write it on the appropriate blank (each answer, 3 points).

barbarians	an isolation	plagues	lost
A.D. 1200-1600	protection	villeins	no
legends	mutton fat	seven	pure
A.D. 400-1500	fief	cold	manor
moats	drawbridge	yes	lord
lords and nobles	dirt	a year and a day	

2.01   About when were the Middle Ages? _____

2.02   Who invaded the Roman Empire? _____

2.03   Most learning was _____ in the Middle Ages.

2.04   Manors were lands given by the king to _____ .

2.05   Because most people could not read they listened to _____ .

2.06   A fief was the land given to the vassal by the _____ .

2.07   Who worked for the town? _____

2.08   What is a quarantine? _____

2.09   A poor man could become free by living unknown in a town for _____ .

2.010 Is pollution a new problem? _____

2.011 If one were a welcome guest, the porter would let down the castle's_____ .

2.012 Castles were built strong for the sake of _____ .

2.013 What surrounded many castles? _____

2.014 Walls were whitewashed every year to cover _____ .

2.015 Soap was made from wood ashes and _____ .

2.016 Lands that can be inherited by the oldest son are called _____ .

Answer the following questions in complete sentences (each answer, 5 points).

2.017 What diseases, that were common in the Middle Ages, are almost unheard of in our country?

_____

2.018 Is pollution a new problem? Explain your answer. _____

_____

_____

2.019   What does good garbage collection have to do with health? _____

_____

_____

Match these words (each answer, 1 point).

2.020 _____ moat

2.021 _____ saltcellar

2.022 _____ tunic

2.023 _____ portcullis

2.024 _____ quarantine

2.025 _____ pumice stone

2.026 _____ sundial

2.027 _____ canopy

2.028 _____ spices

2.029 _____ scullion

a.   bed

b.   movable grating

c.   shaving

d.   spoilage of meat

e.   kitchen help

f.   main item on dining table

g.   man's shirt

h.   protection

i.   tell time

j.   isolation

Answer true or false (each answer, 3 points).

2.030 _____ The root of *supermarket* is *super*.

2.031 _____ The root of *aristocratic* is *aristocrat*.

2.032 _____ The root of *procedure* is *proceed*.

2.033 _____ Often a vowel change is needed when a suffix is added.

2.034 _____ The suffix part of *confessions* is *ions*.

2.035 _____ Pure drinking water helps to keep people healthy.

2.036 _____ Health laws improved after the Romans were defeated.

2.037 _____ London passed an ordinance to prevent people from throwing garbage in the streets.

2.038 _____ *Benedictress* comes before *benedictionary* in alphabetical order.

80/100 **SCORE** _____   **TEACHER** _____ _____
                                            initials   date

3. BOOKS AND SCHOOLS

When the barbarians invaded the European part of the Roman Empire, they destroyed most of the centers of learning. The barbarians looted property, burned books, and destroyed works of art. A thousand years of "Dark Ages" for learning followed. You will learn who the people were who struggled to preserve the few precious books that were saved. You will learn how a few schools were started and how they were different from today's schools. You will be glad to see how good our schools are today.

Section Objectives

Review these objectives. When you have completed this section, you should be able to:

4. Explain the debt we owe the scholars of the Middle Ages.

5. Compare schools of today with those of the Middle Ages.

Vocabulary

Study these words to enhance your learning success in this section.

Benedictine (ben u dik' tēn). An order of monks founded in A.D. 529.

monastery (mon' u ster e). Place where monks live together.

nunnery (nun' ur ē). Place where nuns live together; convent.

parchment (pärch' munt). Specially prepared skins used to write on.

scribe (skrīb). A writer or a professional penman.

university (yü nu vėr' su tē). An association of scholars and students.

vellum (vel' um). Calfskin, lambskin or kidskin used for writing paper.

Pronunciation Key: hat, āge, cãre, fär; let, ēqual, tėrm; it, īce; hot, ōpen, ôrder; oil; out; cup, půt, rüle; child; long; thin; /ŦH/ for then; /zh/ for measure; /u/ or /ə/ represents /a/ in about, /e/ in taken, /i/ in pencil, /o/ in lemon, and /u/ in circus.

BOOKS AND WRITERS

During the Middle Ages and Dark Ages, books were very scarce because they were hand-copied by monks in **monasteries**, especially monks of the **Benedictine** Order. The writers endured cold and suffering to preserve learning. The monks who wrote were also called **scribes**. Those scribes developed eyestrain and rheumatism as they worked to copy many books. Most of their copying was of religious material such as Bibles and prayers. They also wrote the records and stories that were the current events of their day. Writers wrote in the Latin language because it could be understood by all the scholars of Europe, whatever their native language. One of the big libraries of that time belonged to King Richard of England. This library had 280 books. Today, most cities have many libraries, each with thousands of books. Our Library of Congress has 11,000,000 books. What invention made the production of so many books possible?

Materials used in writing were unlike those used today. Yet those dedicated scribes made excellent use of crude materials. They used quills or reeds for pens. They made ink from plants and minerals.

They discovered that bladders of animals were useful for the storage of ink. They used skins of animals for paper. The skin was cleaned and

| Scribes used quills and reeds for pens, and made ink from plants and minerals.

dried into flat "pages." This was called **parchment** or **vellum**. To erase, they scraped the hide with sharp objects. Many of those books, handwritten on parchment or vellum, were very beautiful and were chained to desks for safekeeping.

Scribes also wrote letters for people who could not write. After the letter was written, the parchment or vellum was folded and holes were cut in it so that string could be slipped through. Wax was used to fasten the ends of string together. Then the receiver could tell if his letter had been opened. Another seal told whether the right person had received the letter. Although a few nobles could write their own notes, most peasants could not. Since they had no postal system, messengers delivered the mail.

Complete the following sentences.

3.1 Scribes wrote with _____ .

3.2 Ink was made of _____ .

3.3 Parchment used for paper was made from the a. _____ of b. _____ .

3.4 Erasures were made by _____ .

3.5 Most of the letters were written by _____ .

3.6 Letters were delivered by _____ .

3.7 Books were written in the _____ language.

3.8 Most of the books written in the Middle Ages were about _____
_____ .

Answer the following questions in complete sentences.

3.9 Why would having someone else write your message be dangerous? _____

_____

_____

3.10 Why do you think most of the people could not write? _____

_____

If you wish, you can do one of the following activities.

3.11 BE A SCRIBE.
This would be a good time for you to become a scribe and copy a book or a story.
Or if you wish, you can write your own story. Be sure to make your capitals beautiful with swirls and pictures.

3.12 WRITE YOUR OWN REPORT.
In a reference book or reliable online resources, find out about the printing press.
Who invented the press? When? How do you think this invention changed the way people lived?

SCHOOLS AND TEACHERS

Schools were first established by the Catholic Church to teach the choir boys their prayers and music. One of the most important schools was that of Jarrow at a monastery in England. There the Venerable Bede, who wrote a famous history of England, taught the boys such academics as grammar, numbers, and gardening. By 1100, the monks also taught philosophy and logic. In the **nunneries**, girls learned useful subjects much like our home economics. They cooked, did needlework, cared for the sick, learned music, and sometimes even learned to read and write.

As schools had more and more students, special schoolmasters were hired. To prove their abilities to teach, the instructors had to flog children. In those days, a common belief was that a whipping drove out Satan's evil spirit. For both good and bad pupils to be flogged in memory of the sufferings of others was not uncommon. On December 28, children were flogged to remind them of those children who were killed by Herod. A schoolmaster was an honored person. He sat next to a king or noble at public occasions. He had servants to go with him on his journeys. In his old age, his former pupils took care of him. What do you think of this plan?

Answer the following in complete sentences.

3.13 Why were the first schools started? _____

_____

3.14 Name one great school of the Middle Ages. _____

3.15 Who was Bede? _____

3.16 Contrast the subjects girls learned then and now. _____

_____

_____

3.17 Do you approve of the discipline of the schools in those days? Why or why not? _____

_____

3.18 Why did the instructors whip so often? _____

_____

_____

3.19 Why were good children whipped on December 28th? _____

_____

3.20 Who cared for an elderly schoolmaster? _____

_____

UNIVERSITIES AND SCHOLARS

Universities were formed when groups of learned men lectured to scholars who wrote down what they learned. Sometimes they recited legends. At other times they had such sports as swimming, ball games, and fighting. Most schools also taught how to play musical instruments such as the harp, the flute, or the pipe organ. The students were not governed by the townspeople and often behaved badly. Sometimes the school was forced to move away if the town was displeased. Many famous schools were started. Padua, Naples, Florence, Rome, and other cities had large universities. Gradually a school would become famous for one subject. For example, Paris was famous for theology, Bologna for law, and Salerno for medicine.

Some of the great leaders during this period were men who believed in learning and who did what they could to promote it. In England, King Alfred of the Danes, who began to rule in 871, believed in schools for all. He insisted that books be written in the English language with the exception of math texts, which used Roman numerals. Another great leader was Charlemagne, king of the Franks, who reigned from 768 to 800 in the territory known as France. He was the first Catholic emperor of the West.

Charlemagne strongly urged the clergy to learn how to write correctly. From many countries he secured great scholars to teach. He put his own children in the court school and he himself studied astronomy. He wanted learning for all, no matter the social status, so that everyone would have a better chance to improve their lives. He tried to obey God's command to give equal justice to all people.

Write the correct answer on the blank.

3.21 Name a great ruler of the Danes in England during this period. _____

3.22 Name a great ruler of France. _____

3.23 What numerals were used? _____

3.24 Why did Charlemagne care about learning? _____

_____

Answer true or false.

3.25 _____ University students had no sports in those days.

3.26 _____ University students were governed by the townspeople.

3.27 _____ Some students studied music.

3.28 _____ Salerno was noted for the study of medicine.

Answer these questions in complete sentences.

bene means a prayer   *dict* means to say   *ion* means the act of

3.29 What does *benediction* mean? _____

_____

3.30 When do you hear a benediction? _____

_____

Often a letter or several letters are dropped from a word when a suffix is added.

Complete the root word by adding letters if they have been dropped. Write the suffix.

WORD	ROOT WORD	SUFFIX
dangerous	danger	ous
3.31 famous	_____	_____
3.32 erasable	_____	_____

If a word ends in *y* preceded by a consonant, *y* is usually changed to *i* before adding *es*.

Make this change with the following words.

3.33 monastery _____

3.34 history _____

3.35 victory _____

3.36 century _____

3.37 granary _____

3.38 try _____

3.39 lady _____

Review the material in this section in preparation for the Self Test. This Self Test will check your mastery of this particular section as well as your knowledge of the previous sections.

SELF TEST 3

Write the correct letter and answer on each blank (each answer, 3 points).

3.01   For pens monks used _____ .
a. quills   b. thorns   c. sticks

3.02   Monks made ink with _____ .
a. chemicals   b. plants and minerals   c. minerals

3.03   Ink was stored in _____ .
a. jars   b. bladders of animals   c. skins

3.04   A _____ was an honored person and was cared for by his former pupils in his old age.
a. schoolmaster   b. student   c. writer

3.05   If you went back in time with your present knowledge, you would be considered a learned person because in the Middle Ages most people _____ .
a. could not read or write   b. finished only five grades   c. could read but not write

3.06   The University of Bologna was renowned for the study of _____ .
a. art   b. law   c. medicine

3.07   The University of Salerno was noted for the study of _____ .
a. law   b. medicine   c. art

3.08   Musical instruments taught included the _____ .
a. pipe organ   b. piano   c. guitar

3.09   Messengers delivered letters because they had _____ .
a. slow delivery by mail   b. no postal system
c. mail delivery for the rich only

3.010 Instructors flogged students _____ .
a. only when they were bad superstition   b. to drive out Satan
c. to punish

Answer each question with one or two well-written sentences (each answer, 5 points).

3.011 If all learning today were destroyed, what would you miss the most? (Any answer that is true for you is correct.) _____

_____

3.012 Why were so few books used? _____

_____

3.013 What type of materials were usually written? _____

_____

3.014 Why wasn't the English language used in books? _____

_____

3.015 What is our country's largest library? _____

_____

3.016 Why were children whipped so often in the Middle Ages? _____

_____

3.017 What is a legend? _____

_____

3.018 What was Charlemagne's contribution to education? _____

_____

Answer true or false (each answer, 3 points).

3.019 _____ The scribes suffered from the cold while copying books in unheated monasteries.

3.020 _____ The barbarians destroyed most of the centers of learning when they invaded the Roman Empire.

3.021 _____ Most writers wrote in Latin because it was the easiest language to spell.

3.022 _____ Letters were sealed with strings and wax.

3.023 _____ The first schools established by the Catholic Church were for choir boys.

3.024 _____ Instructors were never allowed to flog students.

3.025 _____ King Alfred insisted that books be written in English.

3.026 _____ Books were handwritten on vellum or parchment.

3.027 _____ King Richard of England had a library of 5,000 books.

3.028 _____ University students studied all the time and never had any fun.

80 / 100   **SCORE** _____   **TEACHER** _____ _____
                                                    initials   date

4. ISLAM

Islam is a religion founded in the late A.D. 600s by a man named Muhammad who claimed to be a prophet. Its followers are called **Muslims**, or Muhammadans. Today, it has more followers than any other religion except Christianity. Its followers spread their religion throughout the Middle East and North Africa by war. Christian Europe had to fight for its very life on several occasions against the forces of Islam. As you study this section, you will learn about the founding of Islam and the fighting between Muslims and Christians. You will also learn the basic beliefs of Islam.

Section Objective

Review this objective. When you have completed this section, you should be able to:

6. Describe the beliefs, origin, and culture of Islam.

Vocabulary

Study these words to enhance your learning success in this section.

abstract (ab′ strakt). Thought of apart from any object or real thing; a form of art that does not look like any real thing.

algebra (al′ je brä). The branch of Mathematics that deals with the relations between quantities. Algebra uses letters as symbols that can stand for many different numbers.

Arabic numerals. The figures 1, 2, 3, 4, 5, 6, 7, 8, 9, and 0.

architecture (är′ ke tek′ chėr). A style or special manner of building.

Constantinople (kon stan tu nō′ pul). A city in Turkey; modern-day Istanbul.

culture (kul′ chėr). The customs, arts, and tools of a nation or people at a certain time.

Koran (kô ran′). The sacred book of the religion of Islam.

Muslim (muz′ lum). A follower of Muhammad; believer in the religion founded by him.

pagan (pā′ gun). A person who is not a Christian, Jew, or Muslim; one who worships many gods or no god; heathen.

Pronunciation Key: hat, āge, cãre, fär; let, ēqual, tėrm; it, īce; hot, ōpen, ôrder; oil; out; cup, pu̇t, rüle; child; long; thin; /ŦH/ for then; /zh/ for measure; /u/ or /ə/ represents /a/ in about, /e/ in taken, /i/ in pencil, /o/ in lemon, and /u/ in circus.

CREATION OF ISLAM

Muhammad was born in the city of Mecca in what is now Saudi Arabia in about A.D. 570. He grew to be a wealthy, well-traveled merchant. When he was about 40 years old he began to have "visions," which he came to believe were the Angel Gabriel speaking to him. This "angel" told him that the word of God revealed to the Jews and Christians was incomplete and mixed up. Muhammad believed himself to be the *only* prophet to receive God's real words, which were later recorded in the **Koran**. The angel did not speak to anyone else, nor were his words confirmed by miracles as in the Old and New Testament. The entire truth of Islam depends completely on the unsubstantiated word of an ordinary, sinful man, Muhammad. However, many people among the **pagan** tribes of Arabia did believe.

These believers were organized into an empire with Muhammad as the ruler. The city of Mecca was named as the center of the new religion. The idols in the city were destroyed, and everyone was ordered to worship the one god, Allah. A large black rock, the Ka'bah, which had been the center of pagan worship in Mecca, became the center of Muslim worship. Even today, Muslims face Mecca in their daily prayers. The people who did not accept the new religion were attacked and conquered. In this way, Muhammad came to rule most of the Arabian Peninsula by the time of his death in A.D. 632.

SPREAD OF ISLAM

After Muhammad's death, the Muslims chose a new ruler. He was called the *caliph*, which means successor. He and the caliphs who followed him fought a *jihad*, or holy war, to spread Islam throughout as much of the world as they could conquer. Muhammad had taught that dying in a jihad guaranteed that a man would go to heaven, so the Muslim armies fought bravely and fiercely. They were very successful.

The Muslim armies swept north and conquered Syria and Iran. They conquered Egypt and the northern coast of Africa. They succeeded in crossing the Straits of Gibraltar and conquered Spain in the early A.D. 700s. Christian Europe was in great danger. In A.D.732, the Muslims attacked France and were stopped at the Battle of Tours. This was one of the most important battles in history. If the Muslims had won, all of Europe would have been open to their armies. However, Charles Martel, grandfather of the great Frankish king Charlemagne, defeated the Muslim armies. God would not allow Europe to fall to the Muslims. However, the Muslims held Spain for over 700 years until the Catholic rulers Ferdinand and Isabella captured the last Muslim stronghold in 1492.

The Muslims continued to spread their Empire to the east. Afghanistan and Pakistan were conquered. Eventually, Turkey and the last remains of the Eastern Roman (Byzantine) Empire were conquered as well. The city of **Constantinople** was captured in 1453. Italy was attacked but never taken.

As they became more powerful, the caliphs became wealthy and lived in great luxury. They became less interested in religion and more interested in their own pleasure. The Empire was divided as Muslims fought among themselves for power. By the 900s, the caliphs were no longer the one ruler of Islam. Great Muslim Empires continued in Turkey, Spain, India, Iran, and Egypt. But, the Islamic world would never be united again.

Answer true or false.

4.1 _____ Muhammad claimed to be a god.

4.2 _____ The Muslims eventually conquered the Byzantine Empire.

4.3 _____ The center of Islam is Mecca in Saudi Arabia.

4.4 _____ The Muslims were never driven out of Spain.

4.5 _____ The Muslim world is still under one ruler.

Answer the following questions.

4.6 Why was the Battle of Tours one of the most important in history? _____

_____

_____

4.7 How was Islam spread? _____

4.8 Why did Muslim soldiers fight so fiercely? _____

_____

4.9 What is the Koran? _____

_____

4.10 What is a jihad? _____

Complete the statements.

4.11 Muhammad claims to have gotten the words of the Koran from _____ .

4.12 The Muslims held Spain for _____ .

4.13 The first ruler of the Muslim Empire was _____ .

4.14 Caliph means _____ .

4.15 The big black rock at the center of Mecca that all Muslims face to pray is called the _____ .

HISTORY & GEOGRAPHY 604

LIFEPAC TEST

NAME _____

DATE _____

SCORE _____

HISTORY & GEOGRAPHY 604: LIFEPAC TEST

Write the correct answer from the list on each blank (each answer, 3 points).

monks	Crusades	identification	cross
Satan	barbarians	Rome	feudalism
protection	Gothic	war	monasteries
plague	fair		

1. Before the invasion, the Western world was ruled by _____ .

2. The Visigoths and Saxons were _____ .

3. In return for work and produce, the lord gave the vassals _____ .

4. Books were handwritten by _____ .

5. The floor plans of churches were often in the shape of a _____ .

6. The system of land ownership in the Middle Ages was called _____ .

7. A once-a-year time of joy was the _____ .

8. Journeys to the Holy Land to recapture it were called _____ .

9. The schools started in the _____ .

10. A disease that destroyed whole cities was called a _____ .

Answer true or false (each answer, 3 points).

11. _____ Manors were independent communities.

12. _____ The villeins belonged to the nobility.

13. _____ Muslims worship many gods.

14. _____ Muslims were taught to be kind to Jews and Christians.

15. _____ The use of money helped trade to develop.

16. _____ People of the Middle Ages had faith.

17. _____ Guilds were started to help nobles.

18. _____ Drama first began under the guidance of the guilds.

Complete the following items (each correct answer, 3 points).

19. The Lords and _____ who fought for a king were given manors.

20. Islam teaches that the last and greatest prophet was _____ .

21. Jews became money-lenders because they _____ .

22. Castles were built on high places for _____ .

23. Most recreation for men was of what type? _____

24. People wanted more luxuries after the _____ were over.

25. Monks who copied material such as Bibles and prayers were also called _____ .

26. Towns liked to buy charters so they could be _____ .

27. St. Francis of Assisi began to preach _____ .

28. Cathedrals were built with great skills because they were houses of _____ .

Choose the right word and write it on the line (each answer, 3 points).

29. An art that made the cathedrals beautiful was that of making _____ .
     a. paintings   b. mosaics   c. stained glass

30. People were beginning to question _____ .
     a. scientists   b. God   c. authority

Write two or three sentences to answer these questions (each answer, 5 points).

31. What was the best characteristic of the feudal system? Explain your answer.

     _____

     _____

     _____

     _____

     _____

     _____

     _____

32. What was the worst characteristic of the feudal system? Explain your answer.

_____

_____

_____

_____

_____

_____

BELIEFS OF ISLAM

Muslims believe in only one all-knowing god, Allah, whom they believe is the creator of all things. Muslims refer to Jews and Christians as "people of the book," believing that they follow some of the truth. Muslims believe that Abraham, Noah, Moses, and many others were prophets. They even believe that Jesus was a prophet, but not the Son of God. They also subscribe to the belief that Muhammad is the final prophet and the only one to receive the entire truth of Allah. The teachings of Islam are found in the religion's central text called the Koran. Early writings, produced by Muhammad in Mecca, preached peace, tranquility, acceptance and inner cleansing through submission to the word of Allah. Muhammad's later writings produced in Medina, however, present a more extreme view and lack of tolerance towards other religions. People interpret Muhammad's teachings very differently, which is why there are three different groups today, just as there are different branches of Christianity. Islam, which means submission to Allah, is based on five basic teachings or "pillars."

They are:

1. Praying five times a day.

2. Believing that there is only one god and Muhammad is his prophet. This is said in a prayer daily.

3. Fasting during daylight hours in the ninth month of the Muslim calendar.

4. Giving alms to the poor.

5. Pilgrimage to Mecca at least once in a lifetime.

Even if a person does all these things and follows the other rules in the Koran, they cannot be sure of salvation. This is called salvation by works. It assumes that people can follow enough of the right rules to earn heaven. Do you think that is possible?

CULTURE OF ISLAM

The Muslim Empires were places of great learning and art. The Muslims honored learning. Muslims of this time usually did not kill or force out the Jews and Christians because they were taught not to harm "people of the book." They were willing to learn from the Jewish and Christian experts in the areas they conquered. This meant that they were able to learn from many sources. Great centers of education were established in the major cities. Baghdad under the caliphs was a city of over a million people with several colleges and a university. Most of the children were taught to read and write.

The books captured during the conquest of the Byzantine Empire were also saved and read. In this way, the Muslims preserved much of the Greek knowledge, which had been kept by the Byzantine Empire. They added to this knowledge becoming experts in medicine, mathematics, astronomy, and other sciences. In time, this knowledge was spread to Europe, primarily through Spain and Italy, as the Middle Ages ended and learning was again encouraged. The Islamic people also passed on to us paper, **Arabic numerals** (Europe was using Roman numerals until then), and **algebra**. Thus, the great Muslim Empires which so threatened Christian Europe came, in time, to benefit them.

Islamic art and **architecture** of this time were very beautiful. Many remarkable buildings and well-planned cities were built all throughout the Muslim world. Muslims were forbidden to draw animals, plants, or people, so they developed beautiful **abstract** designs and lovely forms of writing known as calligraphy. Mosques, centers of worship, were covered with colorful decorated tiles. The Taj Mahal in India is one example of the beautiful buildings the Muslim **culture** produced. During this same period, Europeans were living in primitive homes and few could read or write.

Answer the following questions.

4.16 List three things Europeans received from the Muslims.

_____

_____

_____

4.17 What are the five pillars of Islam?

1. _____

2. _____

_____

3. _____

4. _____

5. _____

4.18 What do Muslims consider Jesus Christ to have been? _____

Complete the following statements.

4.19 The _____ in India is one of the best examples of Muslim buildings.

4.20 Muslim artists were not supposed to draw the _____ .

4.21 Muslim learning eventually spread to _____ as the Middle Ages ended.

4.22 Muslims call Christians and Jews _____ .

4.23 A Muslim center of worship is called a _____ .

4.24 Islamic artists used _____ designs.

Answer true or false.

4.25 _____ Muslims believe that Abraham was a prophet.

4.26 _____ Muslims believe in many gods.

4.27 _____ The Muslims destroyed all of the non-Islamic books they obtained during their conquests.

4.28 _____ Muslims believe there will be more prophets after Muhammad.

4.29 _____ Islamic artists developed a beautiful form of writing called calligraphy.

Complete this activity.

4.30 Read the Bible passages Romans 4:2-5, Galatians 2:16, and Ephesians 2:8 and 2:9.

Write a paragraph about what you think of Islam.

_____

_____

_____

_____

_____

_____

_____

_____

_____

_____

TEACHER CHECK _____ _____

initials   date

Review the material in this section in preparation for the Self Test. This Self Test will check your mastery of this particular section as well as your knowledge of the previous sections.

SELF TEST 4

Write the correct answer from the list on each blank (each answer, 3 points).

caliphs	calligraphy	Ka'bah	jihad	Cordoba
prophet	Mecca	mosque	Muslim	algebra
abstract	Koran			

4.01   The successors to Muhammad were called _____ .

4.02   The black stone that Muslims face to pray is called the _____ .

4.03   The city that is the center of Islam is _____ .

4.04   Abraham was considered by the Muslims to have been a _____ .

4.05   A _____ is a holy war.

4.06   A Muslim center of worship is a _____ .

4.07   The beautiful writing developed by Islamic artists is called _____ .

4.08   The _____ is the holy book of Islam.

4.09   One of the things given to Europe by Muslim cultures was _____ .

4.010   Muslim artists used _____ designs.

Put an X beside the five basic teachings of Islam (each answer, 2 points).

4.011   _____ Fight in all holy wars.

4.012   _____ Give alms to the poor.

4.013   _____ Pray five times a day.

4.014   _____ Pray to Muhammad once a week.

4.015   _____ Pilgrimage to Mecca.

4.016   _____ Believe there is only one god and Muhammad is his prophet.

4.017   _____ Memorize the words of Muhammad.

4.018   _____ Pilgrimage to Jerusalem.

4.019   _____ Pay a special tax for the holy wars.

4.020   _____ Fast during daylight in the ninth month.

Write true or false in each blank (each answer, 2 points).

4.021 _____ Spain was held by the Muslims for less than 50 years.

4.022 _____ Muslims were not interested in knowledge and tended to be unable to read and write.

4.023 _____ Muslim artists were not supposed to draw people, birds, or plants.

4.024 _____ Europeans learned about paper from the Muslims.

4.025 _____ Muhammad died before the birth of Christ.

4.026 _____ Egypt was conquered by the Muslims.

4.027 _____ Muhammad claimed to receive God's word from the Angel Gabriel.

4.028 _____ As the Muslim Empire grew, its leaders remained poor, simple men interested mostly in religion.

4.029 _____ During Muhammad's life, Islam was a peaceful religion spread by preaching and teaching all over Arabia.

4.030 _____ The Muslims destroyed much of the Greek knowledge they found during their expansion.

Answer these questions by putting the correct answer on each blank (each answer, 3 points).

4.031 Muslims call Christians and Jews _____ .

4.032 An important example of Muslim buildings is the _____ in India.

4.033 Jesus is considered to have been a _____ by Muslims.

4.034 Name three countries where great Muslim Empires were established after the Islamic world was divided (1 point each).

_____

_____

_____

4.035 Islam is an example of salvation by _____ because they believe people can earn the right to go to heaven.

Answer the following in complete sentences (each answer, 5 points).

4.036 Why did the Muslim armies fight so well? _____

_____

_____

4.037 Who fought at the Battle of Tours and why was it important? _____

_____

_____

4.038 Who do Muslims believe Muhammad was? _____

_____

_____

80 / 100		SCORE _____	TEACHER _____ _____
			initials　　　date

5. THE CRUSADES

The stories of the Crusades are both heroic and sad. Many courageous deeds were performed, and many foolish mistakes were made. As you study the following section, you will learn that some people went on Crusades sincerely willing to lay down their lives for the Catholic Church. God brought some good things out of this confusion. You will learn what some of these good things were.

Section Objectives

Review these objectives. When you have completed this section, you should be able to:

7. List the reasons for and the results of the Crusades.

8. Explain what we can learn from the Crusades.

Vocabulary

Study these words to enhance your learning success in this section.

Alexandria (al ig zan' drē a). A city on the delta of the Nile and second in importance to Rome.

heretic (her' u tik). One who holds beliefs contrary to others.

Hospitalers (hos' pi tu lurz). An organization of Crusaders who gave medical aid.

Jerusalem (ju rü' su lum). The Holy City; former capital of Judea; what is considered the old city is divided into four quarters: Armenian, Jewish, Muslim, and Christian.

knights (nīts). Men with honorable rank who pledged to do good deeds.

Pronunciation Key: hat, āge, cãre, fär; let, ēqual, tėrm; it, īce; hot, ōpen, ôrder; oil; out; cup, pu̇t, rüle; child; long; thin; /ŦH/ for then; /zh/ for measure; /u/ or /ə/ represents /a/ in about, /e/ in taken, /i/ in pencil, /o/ in lemon, and /u/ in circus.

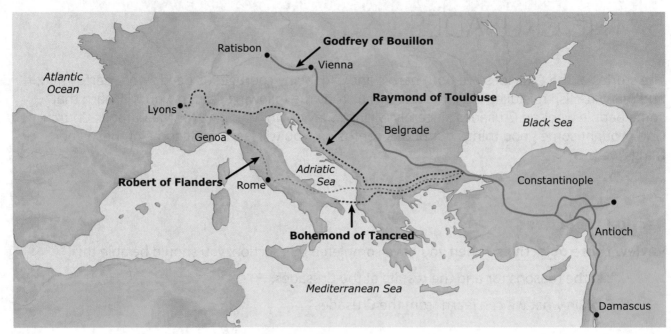

Map 3 | Routes of the First Crusade

THE CRUSADERS

Many people of the Middle Ages were Catholics. They believed in God, the Catholic Church, and their leaders. Consequently, when Pope Urban II in 1095 urged them to make journeys to the Holy Land to win it back from the Muslims, everyone shouted, "God wills it!" Anyone who wished to go could do so. They were excused from debts, prison sentences, or other responsibilities. Crusaders wore red crosses and went in groups. One of the first leaders was Peter the Hermit, who reached **Jerusalem** but did not capture it. The armies under Godfrey, Tancred, and Raymond actually captured Jerusalem and made it into a Catholic kingdom. Before their journey to the Holy Land, these Crusaders had to make a vow.

What kind of vow do you think a Crusader would be required to make before he started on this long journey? A Crusader had to promise to be a good Catholic, and to journey to the Holy Land in the ranks of an organized group approved by the Pope. This vow was binding unless the Crusader was too old, too poor, or too ill. If he were excused, he had to send his son if he had one, or pay the way for a substitute. If a woman desired to go she had to have an armed guard. For proof of success, the first Crusaders brought back holy dust from Jerusalem, but the later Crusaders were required to bring back a letter from someone in Jerusalem. Crusaders, then, were bound by many rules.

The First Crusade was the most successful. The second one was beaten back by the Muslims. Richard the Lion-Hearted lost the Third Crusade, and Constantinople was sacked during the fourth one. In A.D. 1212, a pitiful event took place. A group of 20,000 children left for Jerusalem under the leadership of a ten-year-old-boy, Nicholas of Germany. When the children reached Italy, most of the girls were sold as slaves or became servants to ladies. Boys who went on to the East were sold as slaves. Then another boy, Stephen of France, led a group of 30,000 children. When they reached the city of **Alexandria**, they were sold as slaves and put on ships to be transported. Two ships were lost. Why do you think parents did not object to their children going on these Crusades?

Answer true or false.

5.1 _____ In the Middle Ages people had faith.

5.2 _____ Pope Urban II urged people to go on the Crusades.

5.3 _____ The purpose of the First Crusade was to win back the Holy Land from the Muslims.

5.4 _____ The First Crusade was successful.

Unscramble the answers.

5.5 A Crusader had to obey certain _____ .
srlue

5.6 If he were too old, a man could send his son or a _____ .
busstetuti

5.7 A woman had to have an _____ .
rmead ardgu

5.8 A letter was required for _____ .
oofpr

Answer the following questions.

5.9 Who won the Second Crusade? _____

5.10 Who was Nicholas of Germany? _____

_____

5.11 Who was Stephen of France? _____

_____

5.12 What happened to most of the children? _____

_____

LESSONS FROM THE CRUSADES

Certain groups of Crusaders learned to help other Crusaders. The **Knights** of the Temple protected the Crusaders. The Knights of St. John of Jerusalem, or **Hospitalers**, cared for sick Crusaders. They were trained men. The Order of the Holy Trinity rescued Crusaders who had been captured. Sometimes they offered themselves in exchange for the captives. Crusaders learned about the religions and customs of other people. In particular, they came into contact with the Muslims of the Middle East. As rulers of Jerusalem, the Muslims required Crusaders to follow special rules in order to remain there. They had to pay a yearly fee in gold, place no cross on the outside of any building, and rise if a Muslim entered the room.

The Crusaders found that at least one Arab ruler, Haroun al Raschid, was kind to them.

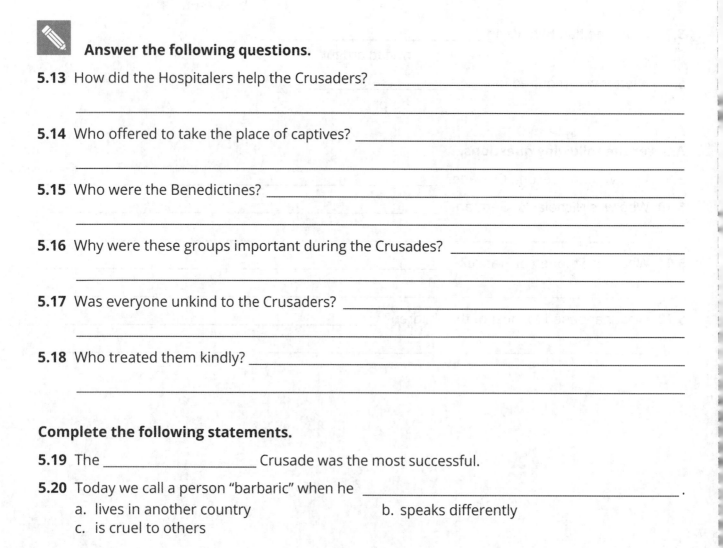

Answer the following questions.

5.13 How did the Hospitalers help the Crusaders? _____

_____

5.14 Who offered to take the place of captives? _____

_____

5.15 Who were the Benedictines? _____

_____

5.16 Why were these groups important during the Crusades? _____

_____

5.17 Was everyone unkind to the Crusaders? _____

_____

5.18 Who treated them kindly? _____

_____

Complete the following statements.

5.19 The _____ Crusade was the most successful.

5.20 Today we call a person "barbaric" when he _____ .

    a. lives in another country   b. speaks differently

    c. is cruel to others

Read Luke 6:27, 28, and 31.

Think about the following questions. Choose one of these questions and write a paragraph on it using complete sentences.

5.21 Do you think the parents of the children who were lost during the Children's Crusades could love their enemies?

5.22 Today many students believe adults should not tell them what they are allowed to do. Can you see why this belief could cause tragedies?

5.23 Have you ever hated anyone who treated you cruelly? How did this hatred affect you? How does the Word of God help you to deal with hatred?

_____

_____

_____

_____

_____

_____

_____

TEACHER CHECK _____   _____
                                    initials   date

THE END AND RESULTS OF THE CRUSADES

Gradually, the people went on Crusades for other purposes. They had become disheartened because of failure, loss of loved ones, and heavy tax burdens to support the Crusades. After that, the Crusades were launched against the peasants in Germany. It became the thing to do—launch a Crusade against one's enemies. Wars were labeled "holy" because they believed it was the duty of Catholics to attack nonbelievers or **heretics**. Crusaders could then forsake their oaths to go to the Holy Land and they could fight at home instead. In Germany, heads of state finally refused requests to crusade because Catholics were fighting each other. The Crusades ended two centuries after they had begun.

Although the Crusades did not accomplish the original purpose, there were several positive results. People learned to be more tolerant of others. They brought back new ideas, new materials for clothing, various cultures, and new spiritual views. Many Catholics began to think that gentle ways should be used to convert souls. Monks gave sanctuary to men of all religions and aided Muslim children who were to be sold into slavery. Sometimes, two religious groups fought side by side and also held their services in the same building. Have you known of similar instances today?

Complete the following statements.

5.24 People learned to be more _____ .

5.25 Crusaders brought back new _____ .

5.26 The monks helped men of all religions and _____ children who were sold into slavery.

5.27 Some Catholics believed war was not the right way to win souls. They believed in _____ _____ .

Answer the following questions.

5.28 Whom did the Crusaders begin to fight? _____

_____

5.29 What do you think of the Crusades? Make your answer personal. Think about things God has told us and how they apply. _____

_____

_____

Complete these activities.

is not = isn't   cannot = can't

A contraction is a shorter way to write two words. An apostrophe is used in place of a letter or letters that have been omitted.

5.30 Make contractions from each of these word groups.

a. we are _____

b. they have _____

c. you are _____

d. I am _____

e. they are _____

f. I will_____

g. do not _____

h. was not _____

i. are not_____

j. did not _____

5.31 Place a number by each word to show its alphabetical order.

a. _____ Pilgrims

b. _____ Pope

c. _____ Muslims

d. _____ parents

e. _____ Crusades

f. _____ Joshua

g. _____ Monks

h. _____ Castilians

i. _____ children

j. _____ Muhammadanism

5.32 A prefix added to the first part of a word changes the meaning of the word. Study these meanings and then write the meaning of each word.

The prefix *dis* means *not*.   The prefix *re* means *again*.

The prefix *in* means *not*.   The prefix *ad* means *toward*.

a. intolerant _____

b. indecent _____

c. rewrite _____

d. reset _____

e. advance _____

f. adjust _____

Review the material in this section in preparation for the Self Test. This Self Test will check your mastery of this particular section as well as your knowledge of the previous sections.

SELF TEST 5

Write the correct answer from the list on each blank (each answer, 3 points).

Castilian	yes	100
our enemies	Crusades	his son or a substitute
Muslim	kindly	faith in God and leaders
vow	thousands	children were shipped as slaves
sick crusaders	no	to take it from the Muslims

5.01   The people of the Middle Ages had much _____.

5.02   Pope Urban II urged them to make journeys called _____.

5.03   Why did they go to Jerusalem? _____

5.04   Was the First Crusade successful? _____

5.05   A Crusader had to make a _____ to do right.

5.06   If a man could not go, he had to send _____.

5.07   Alexandria was second only to Rome as a city, but what dreadful event took place there?

_____

5.08   About how many children went on Crusades? _____

Choose the correct answer and write it on the blank (each answer, 1 point).

5.09   Jesus told us to love _____.
        a. only good people   b. our enemies   c. only people like us

5.010   Should adults who teach you or care for you have the right to make rules for you to follow?
        _____ Yes / No

Complete each sentence using a word from the list above (each answer, 3 points).

5.011   Hospitalers cared for _____ .

5.012   A _____ practices the non-Christian religion of Islam.

5.013   Some barbarians treated the Crusaders _____ .

Answer these questions in complete, well-written sentences (each answer, 5 points).

5.014 Crusaders began to fight for other causes. What were they? _____

_____

_____

5.015 Name at least three ways the Crusades enriched the people. _____

_____

_____

5.016 Would villeins be helpful on a long journey? How? _____

_____

_____

5.017 Were all barbarians cruel to the Crusaders? Explain your answer. _____

_____

_____

Answer true or false (each answer, 3 points).

5.018 _____ There were eight Children's Crusades.

5.019 _____ Many children were captured and sold as slaves.

5.020 _____ Many children finally reached Jerusalem.

5.021 _____ Catholics began to use gentler ways to convert people.

5.022 _____ Monks of the Holy Trinity Order offered themselves in exchange for prisoners.

5.023 _____ Benedictines were scholarly nuns.

5.024 _____ People began to crusade against many other groups.

5.025 _____ The monk scribes kept the light of learning alive during the Dark Ages.

5.026 _____ Most people were careful about sanitary measures.

5.027 _____ The feudal system was, first of all, a system of land distribution.

Complete these sentences (each answer, 3 points).

5.028 True barbarians are those who are _____ .

5.029 King Alfred believed in the _____ language.

5.030 A villein's hut had a _____ roof.

5.031 Jesus would not have approved of war being the center of life in the Dark Ages for He

wanted _____ .

5.032 Venice passed the first _____ .

80/100   SCORE _____   TEACHER _____ _____
                                                    initials   date

6. THE TRADE SYSTEM

At first, the shops of merchants were near the castle. Gradually, they moved outside the walls and clustered in towns. Merchants profited from the demands for luxuries. Guilds were established to protect the craftsmen. Fairs were held once or twice a year to show merchandise and for amusement.

Section Objectives

Review these objectives. When you have completed this section, you should be able to:

9. Describe the growth of towns and trade.

10. Explain the need for guilds.

11. Describe markets and fairs.

Vocabulary

Study these words to enhance your learning success in this section.

apprenticeship (u pren′ tis ship). Learning a trade or an art.

financier (fin un sir′). A person who deals with money.

haggle (hag′ ul). To argue.

journeyman (jėr′ nē mun). A workman qualified to practice his trade.

pigment (pig′ munt). A substance used for coloring.

Pronunciation Key: hat, āge, cãre, fär; let, ēqual, tėrm; it, īce; hot, ōpen, ôrder; oil; out; cup, pu̇t, rüle; child; long; thin; /ŦH/ for then; /zh/ for measure; /u/ or /ə/ represents /a/ in about, /e/ in taken, /i/ in pencil, /o/ in lemon, and /u/ in circus.

MERCHANTS AND GUILDS

Because of the many delightful items seen in foreign lands during the Crusades, people were eager to purchase them; consequently, the merchants profited. Their merchandise included silks, jewels, perfumes, dyes, and unusual fruits. This trade system resulted in the building of shops and the growth of towns. Gradually, a form of money was used because exchange (barter) was too difficult and inconvenient. Merchants who had sufficient money could purchase lands from nobles who needed money to carry on the Crusades or wars; thus, a powerful merchant class developed.

| A jousting knight

Towns. At first, villages of shops and homes grew up around the castles. Then the villages grew and spread outside the walls. Towns made trade easier. They grew bigger in busy places. Sometimes they were near monasteries or churches. Often they developed near important roads or rivers. At first, towns had to pay dues to the lords on whose land they stood. The lords were so eager to obtain money that they sometimes permitted towns to buy charters of freedom. Then the townspeople could manage their own affairs.

Shops. Shops in the town were fire hazards because they were small, flimsy structures. Many carpenter skills and the art of brick-making had been lost. Merchants did not keep materials on shelves, but took orders from their customers. Many merchants lived at the rear of their shops.

Merchants who sold the same type of merchandise tended to build shops on the same street, and the streets were called by the name of the product. If the merchants sold glassware, they lived on Glass Street. If they sold leather products, they lived on Leather Street.

Guilds. Later, each group formed a guild. The guild set up rules and prices for products and services.

Guilds were very important because they took care of families if the guild member died, and they maintained skills at a high level of excellence. Guilds required a young man to serve an **apprenticeship** for several years before he could become a **journeyman**. Then he had to work as a paid assistant, save his money to buy a shop, and produce evidence of his polished skill before he was declared a *master*. After that, he could go into business for himself. Unions today are very much like the guilds.

Money. As the number of shops grew and trade increased, money became a very important tool. Merchants needed to borrow to buy new goods, even as they do today. However, the Catholic Church did not allow its members to lend money at interest. One group of people, the Jews, could lend money because they did not come under the authority of the Catholic Church. Also, many Jews had a good reason to become moneylenders and **financiers**. They had no other way of making a living, because they could not belong to any of the guilds. Guild members were required to take oaths that only the Catholic Church could give.

✏️ **Complete the following statements.**

6.1 The first villages were inside the walls near _____ .

6.2 Then towns began to grow in (name three places) _____
_____ .

Answer the following questions.

6.3 Why did the lords sell charters of freedom to towns? _____
_____

6.4 Why did towns want to buy charters? _____
_____

6.5 Where had people seen new treasures? _____
_____

6.6 Who wanted to sell these beautiful things? _____
_____

6.7 What replaced exchanging goods? _____
_____

6.8 How did money help merchants become powerful? _____
_____

6.9 Did merchants keep products on shelves or take orders? _____
_____

6.10 Where do you think merchants who sold bakery goods would live? _____
_____

Complete these activities.

6.11 For each specialized group, a _____ set prices and made rules.

6.12 First, a young man served an _____ .

6.13 Next, he was a _____ .

6.14 At last, he was a _____ .

6.15 What do you think happened if a member disobeyed the rules? _____
_____

Answer true or false.

6.16 _____ The Catholic Church would not permit money to be lent for interest.

6.17 _____ The Jews did not want to become merchants.

6.18 _____ Non-Catholics could not belong to the guilds.

6.19 _____ The Jews became a class of financiers.

MARKETS AND FAIRS

On market days, which were once or twice a week, merchants set out their products, including produce from the manors. The big events were the fairs, which were held once or twice a year. All the wonderful goods that people desired were on display at booths. They displayed silks and satins, perfumes, carpets, fabrics with golden threads, metalwork, saddles, tablecloths, shoes, **pigment** for paint, dried foods, and fresh vegetables. None of the goods had prices. The custom was that the seller and the buyer would argue over the price. Trading might take hours. Have you ever known this type of **haggling**?

Buying and selling brought much excitement over merchandise at the fairs. Even poor people who could not buy anything enjoyed jugglers, dancers, speakers, singers, and guitar players. Wandering minstrels and beggars related stories and news about other lands they had visited. Now and then, a knight rode through the town on his beautiful horse. Often a noble rode out with his family and attendants. Can you imagine the excitement of a fair day?

Answer the following questions.

6.20 Besides products to buy, what else furnished excitement? _____

_____

6.21 Who brought the news from other lands? _____

_____

6.22 Who might have ridden through the town? _____

_____

6.23 Do we have anything today that is much like the medieval fair days? _____

_____

Answer the following questions or complete the sentence.

6.24 Goods were displayed on market days every week, and at the _____ every year.

6.25 What type of products were sold? _____

_____

6.26 What prices did they have? _____

6.27 Buyers expected to _____ with the seller.

These activities are suggested for extra credit.

On lined paper, write a paper about the fairs. Tell where merchants came from and what they had to sell or trade. What products would you most desire? If you were one of the people who entertained others, who would you wish to be? Compare the fairs then with any you have attended.

Draw a picture of something you would see at a fair. Try to be accurate about the details. Use other pictures or material from books to help you.

Review the material in this section in preparation for the Self Test. This Self Test will check your mastery of this particular section as well as your knowledge of the previous sections.

SELF TEST 6

Answer each item (each answer, 4 points).

6.01   Why were so many arts lost at the time of the barbarian invasion? _____

_____

6.02   Who wrote most of the books and started schools? _____

_____

6.03   Why do you think disease spread so rapidly? _____

_____

6.04   Where had people seen beautiful items they wanted? _____

_____

6.05   What new and powerful class arose? _____

_____

6.06   Why did money come into use instead of exchange (barter)? _____

_____

6.07   If anyone could go to town only once a year, when do you think they would choose to go?

_____

6.08   Who were minstrels? _____

_____

6.09   Why did the merchants start guilds? _____

_____

6.010   Where were the shops at first? _____

_____

6.011   How did having a merchant class help the growth of towns? _____

_____

_____

6.012   How did some merchants become more powerful than some lords? _____

_____

6.013   How were the guilds unfair to the Jews? _____

_____

6.014 Jews became the _____ .

6.015 Before a young man could become a master in a guild, he had to be first

a. _____ and then b. _____ .

Answer true or false (each answer, 3 points).

6.016 _____ Shops were fire hazards because they were built poorly.

6.017 _____ The skills of building had been lost because of the Crusades.

6.018 _____ Products were not displayed on shelves because people seldom wanted to see them.

6.019 _____ Merchants often lived a long way from their shops.

6.020 _____ Each item had a fixed price.

Write the correct answer on the lines (each answer, 3 points).

6.021 Towns were anxious to obtain _____ to rule themselves.

6.022 Guilds of craftsmen were much like our modern workmen's _____ .

6.023 The Catholic Church did not approve of lending money for _____ .

6.024 Instead of bartering, people began to buy with _____ .

6.025 The big event of the year was the _____ .

Write the meaning of the following words on the lines (each meaning, 2 points).

6.026 haggle _____

6.027 journeyman _____

6.028 pigment _____

6.029 apprenticeship _____

6.030 financier _____

7. THE CATHEDRALS

Many beautiful cathedrals built in the Middle Ages are still standing today. Many people worked hard and made sacrifices to build these beautiful structures. Most of these people believed that by helping to build a cathedral they could earn their salvation. However, the Bible teaches that God's grace alone can save us and get us to heaven. (Ephesians 2:8 & 9)

You will learn about the importance of cathedrals and how they were built. You will learn about the way cathedrals were supported financially.

Section Objectives

Review these objectives. When you have completed this section, you should be able to:

12. Explain the importance of the Catholic Church in the Middle Ages.

13. Explain the role of religious drama.

Vocabulary

Study these words to enhance your learning success in this section.

bishopric (bi' shup rik). A church district under the charge of a Catholic bishop.

cathedral (ka thē' drul). The main church of a bishopric.

drudgery (druj' ur ē). Menial work.

indulgence (in dul' guns). A freeing from the punishment one would have gotten for sinning.

mystery play (mis' tur ē plā). A medieval religious play based on the Bible.

ritual (rich' ü ul). A system or procedure.

Pronunciation Key: hat, āge, cãre, fär; let, ēqual, tėrm; it, īce; hot, ōpen, ôrder; oil; out; cup, pu̇t, rüle; child; long; thin; /ŦH/ for then; /zh/ for measure; /u/ or /ə/ represents /a/ in about, /e/ in taken, /i/ in pencil, /o/ in lemon, and /u/ in circus.

| Notre Dame Cathedral

IMPORTANCE

Although most of the people lived in hovels during the Middle Ages, magnificent **cathedrals** towered above many towns. These cathedrals were built to be the main churches of the **bishopric**. Cathedrals represented the faith of the common people in the authority of the Roman Catholic Church, kings, and nobles. Only in the Catholic Church could the poor rise to places of prominence. The **rituals** gave listeners a sense of security, even though the Latin language was not known by most of the people.

| A stained glass window

STRUCTURE

Great cathedrals took many years, sometimes more than a century, to build. Heavy stones, which gave strength to the structures, were carried by men who often gave their labor for no pay. By the twelfth century, the art of making stained glass was perfected and churches were adorned with magnificent windows showing holy scenes. Sand, salt and ashes were heated to make glass. Minerals such as cobalt for blue and iron for yellow were added to make beautifully colored glass. The pieces of colored glass were put together with a solder of lead. During wartime these windows were removed and stored to preserve them. Statues were carved in both wood and stone. Doors were solid and usually carved. The churches were so large that all the people in the surrounding town could attend the same service.

SUPPORT

How were the churches supported in those days? For the most part taxes were used. Sometimes a gift was given to churches because the giver believed the gift would assure them a place in heaven. Bishops owned manors and ruled vassals who had to donate their work. Also, the Catholic Church sold **indulgences**, which were believed to free or delay the punishment of sinners. Kings and nobles gave money, and ladies gave jewels. Because the church was the center of life in the Middle Ages, people had many money-raising projects to finance the building and the upkeep of a cathedral. The entire town surrounding a church used all its talents and crafts to make that building beautiful and flourishing.

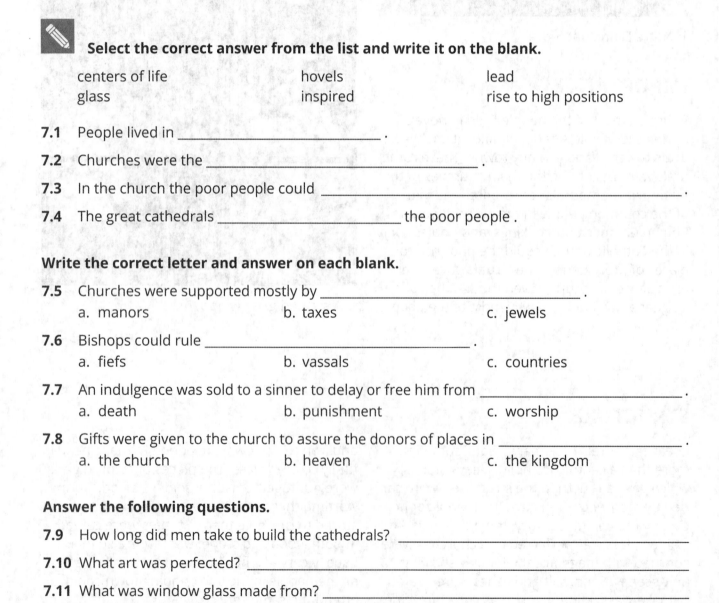

Select the correct answer from the list and write it on the blank.

| centers of life | hovels | lead |
| glass | inspired | rise to high positions |

7.1 People lived in _____ .

7.2 Churches were the _____ .

7.3 In the church the poor people could _____ .

7.4 The great cathedrals _____ the poor people .

Write the correct letter and answer on each blank.

7.5 Churches were supported mostly by _____ .
   a. manors   b. taxes   c. jewels

7.6 Bishops could rule _____ .
   a. fiefs   b. vassals   c. countries

7.7 An indulgence was sold to a sinner to delay or free him from _____ .
   a. death   b. punishment   c. worship

7.8 Gifts were given to the church to assure the donors of places in _____ .
   a. the church   b. heaven   c. the kingdom

Answer the following questions.

7.9 How long did men take to build the cathedrals? _____

7.10 What art was perfected? _____

7.11 What was window glass made from? _____

7.12 How are windows preserved in wartime? _____

DRAMA

Drama began to play an important role in the church services because the people didn't understand the sermons. At first, the priests acted out their messages. Christmas, Easter, and Lent, as well as other special days, were given to dramatic presentations. Because the floor plan of a church was usually the shape of a cross, the play was given in front of the sanctuary. If the play had several scenes, the actors moved up and down the aisles.

Finally, the plays moved outdoors because they had become very elaborate and used much machinery, pulleys, and trap doors. Then the trade guilds took charge. The city council had to approve the scripts, which were expected to follow the Scripture closely, or the guilds were fined. Although the church banned drama, religious plays continued to be used from time to time.

Many kinds of religious plays developed over the years. Besides liturgical drama, which taught stories of the Bible, miracle plays dramatized the lives of saints. **Mystery plays** were based on Scripture. A cycle of mystery plays took several days to show.

Folk plays, which were taken from house to house, included dances and sword fights. Comedies could only deal with evil forces. Farces dealt with the depravity of man. A secular interlude was a nonreligious service between serious church ceremonies.

One popular morality play of the period is still used today. That play is called *Everyman*, which deals with the trials of the average man. Although drama moved out of the church, the themes of faith in God and the wonder of life continued to be found in many great plays for centuries afterwards.

The great cathedrals remained as monuments to the power of a religion that helped people endure the darkness of the Middle Ages. People were beginning to question authority. The lower classes began to rebel against the iron rule and often brutal treatment by the upper classes. In 1208, Saint Francis of Assisi began to preach love and charity for all.

Although no more Crusades took place after the end of the thirteenth century, men wanted to continue traveling and exploring. With the growth of learning, scholars were awakened. The feudal system was coming to an end, and the new and wonderful age of the Renaissance was about to begin.

Write the answers in complete sentences.

7.13 Why did church drama develop? _____

_____

7.14 Who were the first actors? _____

_____

7.15 The floor plan of a church was often in what shape? _____

_____

7.16 Has the church always approved of drama? _____

_____

Select the correct answer from the list and write it on the line.

comedy
liturgical drama
mystery play

Corpus Christi
miracle play
secular interlude

farce
morality play

7.17 The life of a saint was shown in a _____ .

7.18 A story from the Bible was depicted in a _____.

7.19 *Everyman* is an example of a _____ .

7.20 The Scripture was dramatized in the _____ play.

Complete the following activities.

7.21 A synonym is a word that means the same as another word. Write the synonym of the vocabulary word on the line.

aim
entity
select
supernatural

labor
splendid
time period
church

destroy
nonreligious
stimulate
unknown

a. cathedral _____

b. century _____

c. devastate _____

d. drudgery _____

e. inspire _____

f. magnificent _____

g. miraculous _____

h. mysterious _____

i. objective _____

j. secular _____

7.22 If a word ends in *f* or *fe*, form the plural by changing the *f* or *fe* to *v* and add *es*. Write the plural of each word.

knife
knives

a. wife _____

b. life _____

c. leaf _____

d. loaf _____

7.23 If a word ends in *y* preceded by a consonant, form the plural by changing the *y* to *i* and adding *es*. Write the plurals of these words.

    a. authority _____

    b. entity _____

    c. granary _____

    d. holy _____

    e. play _____

    f. pulley _____

Before you take this last Self Test, you may want to do one or more of these self checks.

1.   _____ Read the objectives. See if you can do them.

2.   _____ Restudy the material related to any objectives that you cannot do.

3.   _____ Use the **SQ3R** study procedure to review the material:

    a. **S**can the sections.

    b. **Q**uestion yourself.

    c. **R**ead to answer your questions.

    d. **R**ecite the answers to yourself.

    e. **R**eview areas you did not understand.

4.   _____ Review all vocabulary, activities, and Self Tests, writing a correct answer for every wrong answer.

SELF TEST 7

Select the correct answer and write it on the blank (each answer, 3 points).

7.01   Most centers of learning were destroyed by the _____ .
a. Moors   b. Romans   c. barbarians

7.02   Rome had ruled for about _____ .
a. 200 years   b. 400 years   c. 100 years

7.03   Most books in the Middle Ages were written by the _____ .
a. kings   b. monks   c. knights

7.04   Nobles gave vassals land called _____ .
a. manors   b. fiefs   c. baileys

7.05   The vassal gave the nobles _____ .
a. produce   b. money   c. protection

7.06   Most early castles had walls that were _____ .
a. two feet thick   b. six feet thick   c. eight feet thick

7.07   People ate a great deal of _____ .
a. meat   b. vegetables   c. fruit

7.08   Boys learned to fight when they were only _____ old.
a. fifteen years   b. eleven years   c. seven years

7.09   Of knife, fork, and spoon, the one that would not be on the table in the Middle Ages was

the _____ .
a. knife   b. fork   c. spoon

7.010 Instead of papers, scribes wrote on _____ .
a. linen cloth   b. dried, scraped animal skins

Answer true or false (each answer, 2 points).

7.011 _____ The Crusaders went on their journeys to see the world.

7.012 _____ After the Crusades ended, no one cared to travel.

7.013 _____ Guilds were established to protect the craftsmen.

7.014 _____ Drama began in the church to help actors.

7.015 _____ The church was supported mostly by taxes.

Complete these sentences (each answer, 4 points).

7.016 After the Crusades, the class that grew powerful was the _____ .

7.017 Both amusement and the sale of merchandise took place once or twice a year at _____ .

7.018 Traveling minstrels and beggars told the people _____ .

7.019 Drama outside the church was under the care of _____ .

7.020 The floor plan of most churches was in the shape of a _____ .

Finish each sentence by choosing the correct word and writing it on the blank (each answer, 2 points).

bishopric	money	center	century
sermon in Latin	Hospitalers	stained glass	manor
Venice	Richard the Lion-Hearted		

7.021 One of the big changes in trade was the use of _____ .

7.022 In the Middle Ages the church was the _____ of life.

7.023 A cathedral was the head church in the _____ .

7.024 Drama began in churches because people could not understand the _____

_____ .

7.025 One recaptured art that made the cathedrals beautiful was that of making _____

_____ windows.

7.026 Some cathedrals took more than a _____ to build.

7.027 The knights of St. John who looked after sick crusaders, were called _____ .

7.028 The famous king who lost the third Crusade was _____

_____ .

7.029 A gift of land from a king to a noble was called a _____ .

7.030 The first city to pass a quarantine law was _____ .

Answer each question in one or two well-written, complete sentences (each answer, 5 points).

7.031   What was wrong about the feudal system?

_____

_____

_____

7.032   How did the monk scribes help to preserve knowledge during the Dark Ages?

_____

_____

_____

7.033   What are some of the positive things that came as a result of the Crusades?

_____

_____

_____

7.034   How did the cathedrals help the lives of the poor people?

_____

_____

_____

80 / 100   SCORE _____   TEACHER _____ _____
                                            initials   date

Before taking the LIFEPAC Test, you may want to do one or more of these self checks.

1. _____ Read the objectives. See if you can do them.
2. _____ Restudy the material related to any objectives that you cannot do.
3. _____ Use the **SQ3R** study procedure to review the material.
4. _____ Review activities, Self Tests, and LIFEPAC vocabulary words.
5. _____ Restudy areas of weakness indicated by the last Self Test.